Tomato Frogs as Pets

Tomato Frogs Care Guide

Tomato Frogs General Info, Purchasing, Care, Cost, Keeping, Health, Supplies, Food, Breeding and More Included!

By Lolly Brown

Foreword

Tomato frogs can really be a great pet for new keepers or even for people who doesn't have any experience on handling frogs. They are usually calm and easy going. Before putting into conclusion whether or not this breed might be right for you and your family, you must first make yourself familiar with this frog breed. You have to gather round sufficient information, and devote your time and effort in able to know Tomato frogs well. If you are planning to buy this kind of pet, you must make sure that you are well-informed with its biological information, temperament, and specific needs. You must make sure that you are capable of handling it properly and that you are physically, emotionally, and financially ready in order to become a responsible frog owner.

With the help of this book you'll be able to learn all the necessary information you need to know about Tomato frogs from their heritage, physique, down to their special and specific needs in terms of its health, nutrition, grooming, habitat, maintenance, and well-being. We hope that this book will be of great help for you whether you are an expert or a newbie when it comes to Tomato frogs. Enjoy!

Table of Contents

Introduction

Tomato frogs are usually calm and relaxed. They are primarily terrestrial. They are usually found on vegetation, highly distributed urban areas, coastal forests, rain forest or forests that receive heavy rainfall whenever summer starts or in the latter part of spring. The name "Tomato" was based on their striking colors as females come in a bright red-orange while males have a duller skin that ranges from yellow-orange to brownish-orange similar to the color of a tomato fruit.

This type of frog is most active during the night. Most of the time, they spend the day burrowed under leaves and mud. They are available throughout the year especially during early summer or late spring. Both wild-caught and captive-bred tomato frog shows up in pet trade. Females grow larger than male. Adult males can grow as large as 2.5 inches while females can grow and reach 4 inches measuring from snout to vent. When they are stressed, they secrete a white liquid substance. This is their defense mechanism whenever a predator comes in their way. This can be deadly to others but can only bring allergy to human skin. Unlike cats and dogs, tomato frogs like the majority of the frogs do not enjoy being handled. It is advisable for you to handle your pet frog only when it is needed for instance, when you are going to clean its terrarium

In the following chapters, you'll gain knowledge on the basics of Tomato frog care like its heritage,, temperament and its biological background. You'll also learn how to provide their needs and take care of them with regard to maintenance, nutrition, health, habitat, and breeding. Through this you will be able to see if a Tomato frog is an ideal pet for you.

Chapter One: Biological Information

Before having a conclusion that a Tomato frog is the ideal pet for you, you must first know what kind of amphibian you are about to handle. You must first gain knowledge on all the necessary information you need to know, from heritage down to its needs, in order to check if this is the best pet for you. Having a pet, in general, is a huge responsibility. Make sure that you are capable and ready in all aspect of your life in committing your time, effort, and care to this kind of pet

In this chapter, you'll learn about the general information and biological facts of a Tomato Frog. A list of its sub-species will be given in order for you to choose what would best suit you and your family.

Taxonomy, Origin and Distribution

Tomato Frogs have a scientific name of Dyscophus antongilii.They belong in Kingdom *Animalia*, Phylum *Chordata*, Class *Amphibia*, Order *Anura Family Microhylidae*, Genus *Dyscophus,* and Species *antongilii.*

The natural range of Tomato Frogs is located exclusively on the island of Madagascar down the east coast of Africa. Records show that they are found specifically at Andevoranto, Fizoana, Iaraka, Rantabe, Maroanstreta, Voloina, and Antongil Bay.

It is the largest member among the Microhylid group of frogs. Primarily, they are terrestrial. They are usually found on vegetation, highly distributed urban areas, coastal forests, rain forest or forests that receive heavy rainfall whenever summer starts or in the latter part of spring. They prefer having stagnant or slow moving waterways and ponds around their area.

Tomato Frogs are nocturnal. It means that this type of frog is most active during the night. Most of the time, they spend the day burrowed under leaves and mud.

They are available throughout the year especially during early summer or late spring. Both wild-caught and captive-bred tomato frog shows up in pet trade.

Unfortunately, because of deforestation and an over-collection for the pet trade, this specie has become presently endangered.

Size, Life Span, and Physical Appearance

The name "Tomato" was based on their striking colors as females come in a bright red-orange while males have a duller skin that ranges from yellow-orange to brownish-orange similar to the color of a tomato fruit. Usually, their bellies are yellowish and there are instances that their back and throat have black spots. Their forefeet are not webbed and their hind limbs 'webbing is not that pronounced.

Females grow larger than male. Adult males can grow as large as 2.5 inches while females can grow and reach 4 inches measuring from snout to vent. They can reach the size of an adult after a year if fed well. It takes a minimum of two years for a female Tomato frog to mature.

The average life span of Tomato frogs is 6 years but there are cases wherein they reached 10 years of age. If properly taken care of, their life span can actually be extended.

Sub – Species of Tomato Frogs

Tomato Frogs have three sub species. Read carefully and find out which type of tomato frog will best suit you and your family as well:

Dyscophus antongilii - Madagascar Tomato Frog

Distribution: Madagascar; tropical or subtropical moist lowland forests, swamp, marshes, freshwater

Physical characteristics:

Length: Male 6.5 cm; Female 10.5 cm

Body: Its body possesses an orange-red color which is strikingly vibrant. Females are a lot larger than males. Usually, males have a dull color compared to the skin of the females. Their color act as a warning, that they can be toxic for their potential predators.

Behavior and Nature: When they are under a threat, they secrete glue like substance as an act to deter predators. This can actually produce allergic reactions to human skin.

Dyscophus guineti - False Tomato Frog

Distribution: Madagascar, East coast of Africa

Physical characteristics:

Length: Male 2.5 inches; Female 4 inches

Body: They exhibit a bright and attractive red-orange color giving life to where its name has been derived from.

Behavior and Nature: When they are stressed, they secrete a white liquid substance. This is their defense mechanism whenever a predator comes in their way. This can be deadly to others but can only bring allergy to human skin.

Dyscophus Insularis

Distribution: western and north-western Madagascar dry tropical forest and moist forest

Physical characteristics:

Length: 14 inches to 24 inches

Body: This is a medium-sized terrestrial frog. Unlike other tomato frogs, their color is brown-greyish which are usually symmetrical darker marking is. Males have a dark vocal sac.

Behavior and Nature: Like any other tomato frogs, they secrete a white substance from their body in order to protect themselves from predators. Be careful since whenever they are stressed, they secrete this substance which can bring allergic reactions to your skin.

Quick Facts

Distribution and Range: exclusively on the island of Madagascar down the east coast of Africa; Andevoranto, Fizoana, Iaraka, Rantabe, Maroanstreta, Voloina, and Antongil Bay.

Breed Size: medium-size breed

Body Type and Appearance: Their forefeet are not webbed and their hind limbs 'webbing is not that pronounced.

Length: Adult males can grow as large as 2.5 inches while females can grow and reach 4 inches measuring from snout to vent

Skin Texture: slimy skin

Color: Females come in a bright red-orange while males have a duller skin that ranges from yellow-orange to brownish-orange similar to the color of a tomato fruit. Usually, their bellies are yellowish and there are instances that their back and throat have black spots.

Temperament: When they are stressed, they secrete a white liquid substance. This is their defense mechanism to deter predators.

Diet: captive-cultured crickets and night crawlers.

Habitat: vegetation, highly distributed urban areas, coastal forests, rain forest or forests that receive heavy rainfall whenever summer starts or in the latter part of spring. They prefer having stagnant or slow moving waterways and ponds around their area.

Health Conditions: generally healthy but can be sick from the common illness like Metabolic Bone Disease, Red-leg, and Fungal Infections.

Lifespan: They can live an average life of 6 years but can be further extended to 10 years with proper care.

Chapter Two: Tomato Frogs as Pets

Having a pet is a long-term commitment, and having said that, you must really be physically, financially, and emotionally ready in order for you to keep your pet happy, satisfied, and safe. You must also gain knowledge on how such pet behave before you bring them in your home. You must make sure that both your personality and your pet's will jive.

Through this chapter, you'll be given an overview on how tomato frogs behave as pets. Their temperament will be discussed for you to check whether you can get along with them or not. Points about frog licensing as well as the documents you need to prepare will also be given.

Legal Requirements

If you have the plan to purchase a Tomato frog, you must be knowledgeable not only on their characteristics but also to the certain regulations or restrictions that you have to observe in order to keep them legally. Like in any other pet licensing, the restrictions as well as the requirements will vary depending on the country, region, or state that you belong. It will be better if you consult with any legal authorities near your area. Also, you can do your own research locally or online.

CITES Laws for Frogs

What is CITES?

CITES or the Convention on International Trade in Endangered Species for wild fauna and flora is the one responsible for taking care of plants and animals of different species especially the ones who are considered as endangered. This organization is vocal to their advocacy against over-exploitation of animals and plants through international trade. Roughly 30,000 species of plants and 5,800 species of animals are being protected by CITES.

What continents became a member of CITES?

Majority of the countries belonging in the major continents in the world like Europe, USA, Latin America, Australia, and Asia have become a part of the organization.

What composes CITES?

Convention on International Trade in Endangered Species for wild fauna and flora has 3 appendices. In each appendix is a list of different plant and animal species categorized differently with regard to its rules in exporting, keeping, and trading.

Appendix I is composed of species that are considered as most endangered among any other animals and plants listed by CITES. These species are threatened with extinction.

Appendix II is a list of species that are not necessarily threatened with extinction now but the probability of it depends on how closely controlled the trade is

Appendix III is full of species requested by different parties that regulate trade in the species resulting to the need of cooperation from other countries in order to prevent illegal or unsustainable exploitation.

FAQS: Frog Licensing

Why should I license my frog?

It is advisable for you to have your frog licensed to save you in case of any trouble. Sometime there are veterinarians who checks on the license of the pet in order for them to ensure that you are keeping your pet legally. If you want to travel and planning to bring your frog with you, having it licensed will be a great help since other countries and even airlines are requiring pet licensing before traveling.

What are the requirements for frog licensing?

In general, you don't need to have approval from wildlife organizations or authorities in order to have your frog licensing. All you have to do is to provide a document with the name, identity of the specie on which your frog belongs. There is a need for you to give information like name, address, contact details, and the signature of the previous owner or on where you bought your frog is also needed. You also have to provide your personal information and contact information. This kind of document needs to be kept for future reference for you as the new owner of the frog until it is sold or if it dies.

Does the United Sates require frog licensing?

In the United stated, there is no federal law that mandatorily requires licensing for pets, wild or exotic animals, and amphibians. However, this is being decided on the state level. Therefore, it is highly recommended for you to check on the laws being prevailing in your town, municipality, or state. You may ask the authorities in your area to make sure that you are being able to comply with what is required. Make sure that you'll be able to abide with the rules and regulations in your area to avoid problems in the future.

Ease and Cost of Care

Having pets, in general, can be expensive regardless if it's a low maintenance or a high maintenance one. Either of the two, you need to provide them enough supplies essential for them to keep up with a healthy lifestyle. Though frogs seem like small creatures that are easy to handle and to maintain, the truth is they don't come cheap at all! It is necessary for you to provide everything that your frog needs in order for it to live happy and satisfied.

Though it looks simple, these little things will definitely become an additional line item to your daily budget. The entire cost of these frog-related expenses will vary depending on where you buy the supplies, the brand it belongs, the amount of nutrients present, the time being, etc.

If you want to seriously own a Tomato frog as a pet you should be able to cover the necessary costs it entails. The initial expenses associated with keeping Tomato frogs as pets include the cost of the breed itself as well as the its substrate, accessories, initial medical checkups,, licensing, food, and other equipment needed.

Cage or enclosure, food and water equipment, medical care, cage decor or accessories, materials for breeding, medical care, and the cost of a Tomato frog itself are the overall cost for keeping such specie. It is highly recommended for you to buy only from reputable and legit breeders to ensure that the frog you are going to purchase is healthy and as a much as possible is a captive-bred. You may buy from online stores or websites as well as on amphibian's conventions. Ask for referrals to ensure that you will be able to deal with a well-regarded breeder alone.

Purchase Price: $20 - $50

The cost of a Tomato frog varies. Its price actually depends on its age, color, availability and the breed or specie it belongs to. If you want to purchase a frog with a lower cost you may transact with backyard breeder but at your own risk since if you're going to acquire frogs from them, you wouldn't be so sure that the frogs are well-taken care of or if they are really a captive-bred or have just been randomly captured in the wild. Remember not to purchase a cheap frog if it is in the expense of its health and quality. Tomato frogs, in average, cost $20 to $50. Usually, the younger ones are being sold at a lower cost than the adults.

Terrarium and Screen Lid: $20- $40

A frog needs its own place to stay in order to feel relaxed, safe, and comfortable. It is ideal for you to mimic its natural habitat for it to be able to adjust easily on its new surroundings. In buying a cage, make sure that it is appropriate for the size and age of your frog. The enclosure should be made out of glass so that you can easily monitor your pet, regulate temperature, and for the reason that this kind of cage will be easier to clean. You may buy an enclosure along with a screen lid for as low as $20 but it greatly varies depending on the size, brand, and quality of the cage. The cost of it can further increase up to $50

Food, Water Dish, Tank Heater: $20- $35

Tomato frogs can be fed by gut-loaded cricket. There is also a need for their food to be dusted with calcium powder as they need the mineral for them to avoid developing certain diseases. You also need to provide them with water at all times. Temperature and humidity inside the cage should be properly maintained. Therefore, tank heater along with thermometer and hygrometer will be needed.

Veterinarian Consultations: $75 - $100 or more

It is advisable for your pet to visit the vet once in a while for a routine check-up in order to make sure that its health is exceptional. Just like humans, Tomato frogs can also get sick. They may potentially carry different diseases without you knowing it. And so, you need to save up for its medical needs and veterinarian costs. You should also save a budget for medical or lab tests just in case your frog will need such procedures

Supplies/Accessories: $10- $15

In order to simulate a healthy environment for your pet, you should be able to set up its terrarium as if it's living in the wild. You may add cage decors such as branches, leaves, live plants, moss and other things that would make the cage pleasing to the eyes. It is up to you what supplies or accessories to use. Just make sure that you will not overdo it.

UVB Lighting and Gauges: $50 and up

It is not really that necessary for Tomato frogs to have access on UVB Lighting but having one won't hurt. If ever you will add a plant inside the cage, the UVB lighting will be a great factor for it not to wither. UV lighting is not really required for Tomato frogs but using one would benefit your pet as it can help the frog process calcium and other vitamins that are beneficial for its health.

Chapter Three: Purchasing and Selecting a Healthy Breed

After knowing all the legal requirements as well as the temperament of this amphibian, it's now time for you to be able to know where and to whom should you acquire a healthy breed of a Tomato Frog. This part can be very crucial as this the time wherein you're going to choose the pet you're going to spend the rest of your time with.

In this chapter, we'll help you depict whether the breeder you are dealing with is reputable or not. Plus, we'll give your ideas on where you can buy a Tomato frog. Through reading this chapter, you'll also learn how to determine a healthy frog from an unhealthy one.

FAQS: Buying a Tomato Frog

Where can I purchase a Tomato Frog?

- Backyard Breeder

  There are lots of backyard breeders selling Tomato
  Frogs. Buying from them may look appealing as they
  really know how to persuade customers but you must
  take precaution and think twice before buying. You
  cannot be certain on the health of the frogs in their
  custody. There's a chance that these frogs are illegally
  imported from the wild that may suffer from poor health
  conditions resulting from importation damages. Frogs
  who have lived in the wild may face problems when
  they have been captured. It may face difficulty in
  adjusting to its new environment. Make sure that the
  backyard breeder you are transacting with has a good
  reputation.

- Local Pet Stores

  You may check on the nearest pet store in your area if
  they are selling Tomato Frogs. Be sure that the store has
  provided a good living condition for the frog. If not, do
  not think twice and leave. If the frog has been kept in a
  not so good environment there's a chance that it is

infected with certain diseases. It is not recommended for you to buy in pet stores since it is believed by some animal groups that their industry is made to make profit out of the expense of these wild animals.

- Amphibian Convention

  This type of convention is exclusively made for amphibian enthusiasts. In here you can meet reputable sellers and other frog owners as well. You can get referrals from other patrons in order for you to now to whom should you purchase a frog. This is not a daily event. You have to wait for months or years before another convention will be held in your place.

  Reminder: Always ask for referrals before dealing with breeders. There are several forums online on which they are giving reviews and recommendations of several breeders.

What kind of Tomato frog should I purchase?

It is advisable for you to acquire a captive bred frog. This kind of frog may be a little costly but it will be more economical in the future. If you purchase a captive bred frog, you can be sure that they have been taken care of properly. There is no chance that they are carrying any in illnesses which can save you bucks from medical expenses. They can easily adapt to the new environment they belong to compared to those that have been captured in the wild.

Is there a need for me to quarantine my frog?

There's a possibility that the frog you have purchased is carrying diseases that may not be harmful to them but may potential affect you and your other pets as well. It is the main reason that you must have your frog under quarantine for a few days. This process is not really required especially if you really trust the breeder you have dealt with but if not; it is a good way for you to ensure the health safety of everyone in your house.

There are lots of factor that may affect the health of your frog. Stress from shipment and traveling can trigger a hidden disease they carry. The food that they ate before being captured is a factor as well if ever they have been caught from the wild.

Quarantining your Tomato Frog is done in order to diagnose if your pet is suffering from infection as well as to assess the health condition of your pet. It is the way to ensure that the frog you have purchased is not carrying any transmittable diseases. From this, you can prevent any sickness to be transferred to the whole household.

In order for you to have a successful quarantine period for your Tomato frog, first you need to provide a properly sanitized quarantine tank. A 10 to 20 gallon aquarium can be used. You may use sphagnum moss as the substrate of the vivarium as it holds more moisture and provides a nice hiding place for the frog. Make sure that your frog has access to water at all times. Monitor the humidity and maintain the cleanliness inside the cage. After setting up the tank, place your frog inside it. Make sure that your hands are clean before and after handling them. Let your frog stay inside the quarantine tank for at least 45 days. You may bring a sample of your pet frog's fecal sample to your veterinarian and have it tested.

Steps in Finding a Reputable Breeder

Finding a well-regarded breeder can be a little bit challenging and yet it is very necessary. It is essential as they mirror the kind of upbringing the frog had. If the breeder is responsible and caring, you can be sure that the frogs they have bred were raised in a healthy environment.

Here are the following steps for you to be able to choose a reputable Tomato frog breeder:

Step 1: Investigate

Detective mode on! Bring out your magnifying glasses as we are going to make a little investigation towards the breeder you are about to deal with. Doing a background check is the initial step. See to it if the breeder has a website if so the investigation shall begin. Check the content of the website. Make sure the complete contact information as well as the facilities of the breeder is shown. Look for licenses, registrations, and other documents proving that they are selling frogs legally. If the website of the breeder seems suspicious, leave the site and just find another legitimate breeder.

Step 2: Interview

You may try to contact the breeder through phone and conduct an interview. You may ask for their experience with regard to taking care of a Tomato Frog and how long they have been breeding Tomato frogs. See to it if the breeder offers health guarantees. You can ask information about the frog's registration and health information. You may ask questions. One great sign that the breeder you are having a conversation with a reputable breeder is when he ask about you as well. A good breeder would ensure that the frog he bred will be transferred into good hands,

Step 3: Inspect

You may request for an ocular visit inside the facilities of the breeder. If he allows you to do so, it means that they aren't hiding anything and confident that he is taking care of the Tomato frogs well. Inspect the area where the frogs have been raised. Observe the surroundings and makes sure that it is clean and pleasant. If the environment seems unhygienic and unorganized, do not deal the breeder.

Signs of a Healthy Tomato Frog

After you learn how to determine a reputable breeder, it is now time for you to know what signs to look for in order to choose a healthy Tomato Frog:

- The skin should be bright and clean. It shouldn't have scratches, lumps, dryness, and irritations.

- The eyes should be clean and free from any haziness or cloudiness as these may indicate a disease.

- It should be active. Signs of being bloated, lethargic, and lazy should not be present

- The frog should look enthusiastic. It should be able to eat properly during "feeding time."

List of Breeders and Rescue Websites

There are lots of breeders who have their own website for you to visit. If you are planning to buy a Tomato Frog, you may check on the internet in order for you to make sure that you are going to be dealing with a well-regarded frog breeder. To make it easier for you, we have provided a list of frog breeders and rescue websites.

Breeders and Rescue Websites

Back Water Reptiles
<http://www.backwaterreptiles.com/frogs/tomato-frog-for-sale.html/>

Snakes at Sunset
<http://snakesatsunset.com/baby-tomato-frogs-for-sale/>

Reptile City
<http://www.reptilecity.com/Merchant2/merchant.mvc?Screen=PROD&Product_Code=TFL/>

Pet Solutions
<https://www.petsolutions.com/C/Live-Frogs/I/Tomato-Frog.aspx>

ReptMart
<http://www.reptmart.com/p-2151-tomato-frog-for-sale.aspx/>

Underground Reptiles
<https://undergroundreptiles.com/shop/large-tomato-frog/>

Frog Forum
<http://www.frogforum.net/showthread.php/6062-Breeding-false-tomato-frogs/>

Herp Center
<https://www.herpcenter.com/threads/breeding-the-false-tomato-frog.22932/>

Exotic Pets
<https://www.exotic-pets.co.uk/frogs-and-toads-for-sale.html/>

Amphibian Rescue & Conservation Projects
<http://amphibianrescue.org/tag/tomato-frog/>

Smithsonian's National Zoo & Conservation Biology Institute
<https://nationalzoo.si.edu/animals/tomato-frog/>

Amphibian Ark

<http://www.amphibianark.org/tomato-frog/>

Wilmette Pet Center

<http://wilmettepetcenter.com/2011/10/16/tomato-frog-care/>

Chapter Four: Habitat Requirements for Tomato Frogss

Setting up the environment you'll let your frog live in seems to be complicated but you don't need to worry as it is not hard as it seems. All you need to know is the basics on how to prepare an enclosure as well as what materials should you provide for your frog along with the proper place you should put them on.

We've got you covered! Through this chapter will give you a step by step procedure on which you can make use of as guide when you are setting up your pet's cage. We'll give you a list of all the necessary materials you need in order to replicate the environment your frog got used to so that the comfort level that it brings will be exceptional. Ways on how you'll be able to maintain the cleanliness of your pet's enclosure will also be provided.

Habitat Requirements for Tomato Frogs

Like any other pet, your Tomato frog needs its own space on which it will feel comfortable, relaxed, and secured. In setting up a habitat for your pet, make sure that you are able to replicate the environment it naturally belongs in order for it to easily adjust with its new home. In order to make it all possible, you have to know the things you need to prepare in order to set up a cozy place for your frog to stay.

Below are some of the things you have to consider in providing an enclosure for you Tomato frog:

Cage

For every Tomato frog you own, you must provide a 10-gallon aquarium. Although this size of enclosure can house two adult Tomato frogs, it is still advisable for you to provide a larger one if you are letting them live together. Examples of the sizes are as follows: 1 frog- 10 gallon aquarium; 2 frogs - 20 gallon aquarium; 3 frogs - 30 gallon aquarium. It is recommended for you to just separate the frogs instead of letting it leave together for them not to be stressed out with each other's presence.

For tadpoles, provide them a glass terrarium with a screen lid on the top. There is a need for you to change the level of temperature inside the cage and so buying a glass cage is more preferably than a plastic cage that can be bought from pet store.

Substrate

Tomato frogs love to burrow. It will be a must that you provide them with a substrate that will allow them to do their favorite thing. You may use soil, sphagnum, river sand, and coconut fiber. Provide at least 2 inch with regard to the depth of the substrate. If you are going to use soil, make sure that it is free from any chemicals like pesticides, herbicides, and fertilizers. Once it has been placed inside the cage, spray it down with clean water. Be sure to replace the entire substrate once or twice a month and be able to mist it with de-chlorinated or stale water once or twice daily.

Hiding Spot

Make sure you'll be able to provide a hiding place for your frog. You may use a half-branch log tunnels that can be bought in local pet stores. Ensure that the size of the hiding spot is appropriate for you frog.

Accessories and Accents

It is very important that you'll be able to mimic the natural habitat of Tomato frogs. Adding plants can keep your pet feel secure and comfortable. You may add fake plants or even real plants such as Pathos. If you are planning to use plants to decorate the cage of your pet, make sure you'll put them in small pots since Tomato frogs love to burrow and they might hamper the plant's growth. The accessories you're going to use depend on how you want its new home to look like. This part entails creativity and imagination. Make sure not to overdo it. Save some space for your frog to explore.

Water Bowl

A water bowl is essential for your frog's hydration. You should provide a large but shallow water bowl for your Tomato frog. Its depth should not be higher than the height of your pet when resting in order to avoid the risk of drowning. Place the water bowl on the warmer side of the cage so that when it gets cold the water will not be too cold for it. The types of water that you may provide for your Tomato frogs are the following:

- Tap water that have been left sitting for 24 hours without being covered in order for the chlorine to evaporate
- Bottled water
- De-chlorinated water

Make sure that the water bowl should be cleaned in a daily basis. Always check on the level of water inside the bowl and refill it if there's a need to.

Cage Setup Guidelines

It's not only the tangible things that are essential for the habitat requirement of Tomato frogs. Factors such as the temperature, humidity and ting should also be considered. Below are some points you have to follow in order to provide the best home for your pet.

Temperature

The temperature inside the cage should be maintained at 75 to 85 degrees Fahrenheit during the day and 65-75 degrees Fahrenheit during night time. During winter, if the ambient temperature falls below 65 degrees Fahrenheit there is a need for you to use a thermostatically controlled heat pad beneath the enclosure of your frog.

The best way to measure the temperature is by installing a thermometer inside the cage. Always keep track of temperatures because when it reaches higher than 80 degrees Farenheit, it might cause the death of your frog.

Humidity

Humidity can be maintained through the process of misting the enclosure twice daily- in the morning and during the afternoon. Putting a water bowl inside the terrarium can help bring up the humidity inside. Through the help of ventilation humidity can be maintained. The humidity level of the cage should be 70% to 80%. The best way to measure humidity is through a digital hygrometer.

Lighting

Although lighting is not essential for tomato frogs, there is still a need for you to install spectrum bulbs such as fluorescent tubes in order for the live plants to grow. UV lighting is not really required for Tomato frogs but using one wouldn't hurt as it can help the frog process calcium and other vitamins that are beneficial for its health.

Cage Maintenance

Cleanliness inside the cage should be maintained at all times. When cleaning the cage, make sure that you will first put your frog in a separate cage for its safety as we want to avoid them from ingesting harmful chemicals,

Put out the old substrate. Use a detergent soap or bleach in cleaning the cage. Use a sponge and scrub the enclosure gently to avoid scratching it. Rinse it thoroughly and make sure it's free from soap or any substance you have used for cleaning it. Let it completely dry.

Set up the substrate along with the other accessories and equipment then place your frog inside its newly cleaned terrarium.

Remember that a clean enclosure will help your Tomato frog prevent catching any illnesses caused by germs and bacteria. Do this at least once a week or every other day.

Chapter Five: Nutrition and Feeding

Health is wealth. Keeping your pet healthy will also keep you from spending money. Health is something that should never be compromised and should always be prioritize as it is where the life expectancy of your frog depends on. The food you are providing as well as the supplements you are administering to your frog plays a vital role to its health and nutrition. Factors such as body, age, and level of activity are usually considered in order to determine the correct nutritional needs of your pet.

In this chapter, you'll be given some guidelines on what kind of food and how often should you let your Tomato frog eat. Tips on how to properly feed your pet frog will also be discussed.

Nutritional Needs of Tomato Frogs

The health of your pet is something you should prioritize as it is where their life expectancy relies on. Usually, Tomato frogs can live an average life of 6 years but there are cases that they reached the age of 10 years old. With proper diet and nutrition, your pet can also reach this age. For this reason, you should be able to watch what your pet eats. In the wild, they can eat as much as they like and whatever they catch but being a captive-bred the items in their food list that you can provide have somehow become limited. If you want your pet's lifespan be extended, make sure you are able to provide all their nutritional or dietary needs.

Basic Feeding Ingredients

Nutritional Needs of Tomato Frogs

Tomato frogs in the wild live only at a maximum of 4 years, but in captivity, they live for about 10 – 15 years in general, the main reason is because of their nutritional diet. The main reason for it obviously, is because these wild caught frogs don't have proper nutrition compared when they are being taken care of. They usually eat fish, huge insects, other frog breeds (sometimes their own kind), worms, as well as small reptiles, amphibians and mammals such as mice. The predator – prey factor in their natural habitats is also a major cause of their short lifespan.

Basic Feeding Ingredients

Tomato frogs are considered carnivores and insectivores. Their primary diet is consisted of small roaches, crickets, silkworms, night crawlers, horn worms, and other types of insects and worms. They can also eat rodents. It is recommended that the meal you provide for your pet varies for a more balanced nutrition.

Every meal you will serve to your frog should be dusted with the following supplements:

- Every other feeding - Calcium without D3

- 3 to 4 times a month - Calcium with D3

- 3-4 times a month - Multivitamins

These vitamins and supplements is necessary for bone growth especially for growing tadpoles. Make sure that the right amount of these vitamins will be served to your pet. You may ask for your veterinarian's instructions with regard to this matter.

You may provide pre-killed mice or rodents to your pet occasionally but you think twice. Studies show that these preys are low in calcium and high in fat which is not healthy and recommendable for your frog to consume. Experts and veterinarians said that feeding them with mice may cause to certain deficiencies and obesity as well as resulting to a shorten lifespan.

Feeding Amount for Tomato Frogs:

Juveniles or the younger frogs could be fed for 5 to 7 times a week. On the other hand, adults should be fed for 3 to 4 times a week or every other day. The amount of food you should serve depends on the size of your tomato frog. If ever you have more than one frog inside an enclosure, see to it that both is getting an ample amount of food. Do not give them more than what they can handle

For tadpoles and young frogs, there is a diet called gut-loaded diet that you may want to administer in order to strengthen the body of your pet as well as its immune system against any illnesses as it grows.

What is Gut - load Diet?

Gut-load diet is the process of increasing the nutritional value of the prey that you are going to feed your pet 48 hours before you serve it to them.

We all live in an ecosystem and we all benefit from each other one way or another. A good example is the food chain. In which an animal preys on another animal and eventually the predator becomes the prey of another animal as well. The nutrients contained by the prey will pass on to its predator and so on.

In captivity, it is impossible for you to create the same natural cycle present in the wild but gut loading can be an alternative in order to replicate this process.

By this way, if you feed high nutritional value food to the prey you are about to serve, your pet will also receive the nutrients you have loaded to its meal. Make sure that the right kind of vitamins or nutrients will be passed in order to achieve balanced nutrition

Usually, in order to successfully gut load the prey you are providing, there is a need for you to administer multivitamin powder with calcium. Be mindful that phosphorus inhibits calcium absorption therefore the level of calcium should be higher than the phosphorus level. Its oxalates content should also be at minimum.

Most commercial gut loads you can purchase are low in calcium which may not be enough for the nutritional needs of your frog. Do not worry since you can formulate your own gut loading recipe. By this way you can save money and really make sure that the nutritional content will be exceptional

Below are the steps you can make use of in choosing the right ingredients for your gut load formula:

Step 1: Choose what kind of food you are going to use for gut loading your frog's food. You may choose between fruits and vegetables. Have at least 2 or 3 options. Serve it alternately every now and then.

Step 2: Make sure that the fruits and vegetables of your choice are free from any chemical residue like pesticides. Rinse it thoroughly under fresh running water. These chemical components can be toxic to so make sure the foods are properly rinsed.

Note: The nutrient content of the prey you have gut loaded will pass on your frog after 2 to 3 weeks of consuming.

The ingredients in gut loading should be high in calcium content and low in phosphorus, goitrogens, and oxalates. Food like dandelion leaves, collard greens, mustard greens, escarole lettuce, watercress, papaya, alfalfa, and turnip greens are just some of the components you should primary consider as their nutritional value fits with what has been required. You may also mix it with ingredients such as sweet potato, orange, carrot, kale, butternut, squash, black berries, bok choy, green beans, and apples but the calcium content of these ingredients are only in the moderate level though they are still relatively low in oxalates, goitrogens, and phosphorus.

For a more well-rounded and balanced nutrition, you may mix both the primary and secondary ingredients with dry gut-loading ingredients. These ingredients include dried seaweed, bee pollen, sunflower seeds (unsalted and organic), almonds (unsalted and organic), flax seed, and spirulina.

Avoid using food with low calcium content as it will only be a waste since calcium is the kind mineral you want for your frog. Food such as potatoes, oats, meat, eggs, beans, cabbage, romain lettuce, spinach, iceberg lettuce, cat food, dog food, broccoli, grains, corns, tomatoes, fish food, and canned dead insects should not be used for gut-loading.

Carnivore Diet

If you provide a carnivore or meat diet for your pet, it might cause choking as it might be larger than their digestive system. It is recommended that you feed your pet with gut-loaded insects. By this way they will be able to receive all the nutrients they need without the risk of suffocation.

Calcium

Tomato frogs need a generous supply of both vitamins and minerals. The most important vitamins you should provide for your frog is calcium. In order to make this possible, you may dust the food you are serving to your frog with calcium powder.

Calcium is a kind of mineral necessary for proper bone growth and development. It may prevent diseases such as Metabolic Bone Diseases which is very common and fatal to frogs. Deficiency in this mineral can result to broken bones, crippling, and death.

How to Properly Feed Your Tomato Frog

Below are some guidelines on how you will properly feed your tomato frog:

- **Check the nutritional value:** Make sure that you are providing the best food for your pet. See to it that they will receive enough vitamins and minerals

- **Gut-load the prey:** If you are going to feed your frog with insects, it is advisable that you gut load its food first with ingredients that is high in calcium and low in phosphorus, goitrogens, and oxalates.

- **Establish Meal Schedules:** Be sure that you are following the right schedule when to feed your tomato frog

- **Do not overfeed:** Make sure that the amount of food you are providing for your frog would only be enough. Do not overfeed it as it may cause several digestive problems.

- **Use thong if you aren't used to touching insects:** It is under your discretion if you are going to hand-feed your frog. If you aren't comfortable with handling insects, you may use thong s or any other tools in feeding your pet.

Chapter Six: The Life cycle of Tomato Frogs

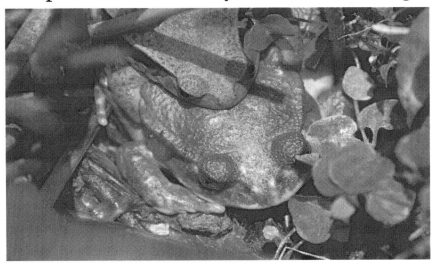

Like humans, Tomato frogs undergo series of stages before they reach adulthood. They start to exist as a teeny tiny egg and eventually grows into these exotic and yet beautiful colorful species. It is very amazing how life works. How a single egg can turn into a creature such as this.

To further introduce you to this amphibian, we'll give you a ride on the stages it faces before it reaches adulthood. You'll be able to discover what happens as each stage passes and you'll understand how metamorphoses really work. This is going to be an interesting journey so buckle up as we give you the life cycle of Tomato Frogs.

Reproduction

Tomato frogs are considered polygynandrous when it comes to mating like most anurans. In some breeding programs for captive-breds, males are found to be calling and amplexing females under simulated heavy rainstorms just like what they use to have in Madagascar. Being able to replicate the environment they got used to will help them adjust and do the process of reproduction easily.

Studies show that at all months during the wet and dry seasons of Madagascar, males do call for mates. Most studies agree with that heavy rainfall events are what trigger the frogs to mate. And so, this condition should be considered if you are going to breed your Tomato frog. After calling out for mates and finding a match, the male will cling to the female or will undergo the so-called amplexing. After that you may expect 1500 eggs per clutch. Eggs that have been fertilized will be deposited on stagnant water or in small ponds. It may take up to 36 hours before these eggs hatch

The Eggs or Frogspawn

The eggs are enclosed in a jelly-like substance which protects them until they hatch. It is usually sticky and comes into a black and white color. They will fall directly to stagnant water or small ponds and will look like a film over the surface of the water. Each egg comes in the size not larger than 2 mm. After 3 days, these fertilized eggs will turn into small tadpoles. The more eggs the frog lays, the more chances that some of them will survive.

When fertilized eggs clump together as they stream in the water they are called frogspawn. For a fact, larvae are able to detect or sense nearby predators through vibration and to save themselves from being eaten, the eggs will hatch earlier than the usual time for hatching. This process on where embryos or eggs hatch early in order to protect themselves is called phenotypic plasticity.

Larvae or Tadpoles

Tadpoles are only a half centimetre in length making them a welcome prey for animals larger than them. They resemble so much of a fish's physique as they also use their tails for swimming and their gills for breathing. This stage will usually last for 7 to 9 weeks.

They feed on tiny bits of nutrients found in water through the use of filtration. As they mature, they will develop small legs that will help them emerge from water and crawl towards the land. Its tail will eventually shrink as apoptosis takes place on which the cells die which results in the reabsorption of the body parts or organs. Their lungs will also begin to develop as their gills disappear. Their eyes will also be repositioned and the formation of eyelids will be present. Their skin will become tougher and thicker. Body parts such as its tongue and jaw will start to form.

After the tadpole has completed the process of apoptosis, it can now become terrestrial and move into places in the fashion of powerful leaping with the use of the suction cups found on their toes. Usually they hide under the plants or burrow themselves under mud.

Froglets or Young

Tomato frogs can really be a great pet for new keepers or even for people who doesn't have any experience on handling frogs. They are usually calm and easy going. Before putting into conclusion whether or not this breed might be right for you and your family, you must first make yourself familiar with this frog breed.

Small Tomato frogs or froglets are somewhat yellow in color. This stage is where they become terrestrial species and explore the environment outside water. When they mature, their color start to change into a yellowish-orange depending on the specie it belongs. Their body size will gradually increase as time goes by.

Adult Frogs

It takes almost a year before a frog totally matures but in the case of a female Tomato frog, it takes a minimum of 2 years before it becomes a fully-grown adult, when this happen you can easily see the difference through its color and size. Females grow larger than male. They can grow up to 4 inches while an adult male can grow as large as 2.5 inches. Their color ranges from bright yellowish-orange for females to dull brownish orange for males. Usually they will have black spots under their throat. They will stay on rainforests, vegetation, or even on highly distributed urban areas.

After they have become mature frogs, the process of reproduction may now occur and the cycle will go back to stage 1.

Chapter Seven: Caring Guidelines for Tomato Frogs

Your pet can be a little aloof especially during the first week of its stay. With proper socialization, your frog will surely get use to you being its new owner. Do not force it to be okay right away, let it adjust for quite some time and surely it will get used to its new environment in no time.

Through this chapter we'll give you tips on how you'll properly deal with your pet frog. Answers to some of the most frequently asked questions with regard to the temperament of Tomato frogs will be given along with the guidelines on how to take care of them. Facts about this specie will also be provided.

FAQS: Temperament of Tomato Frogs

It is essential for you to know how your potential pet behaves in general. In this way, you'll be able to see if your characteristics match well with a Tomato Frog. You must really gain knowledge on its temperament of behavior for you to know what to expect when you already own one. Having a pet is a long-term commitment. Therefore, you must really know what kind of pet you are about to deal with. From this way you'll learn how to take care of them properly.

To help you know more about Tomato frogs, we have answered for you some of the most frequently asked questions with regard to its behavior.

How do Tomato frogs behave in general?

Tomato frogs, in general, are calm and easy going frogs. They are nocturnal which means they are most active during nigh time. They are considered as one of the noisiest types of frogs as they do "ribbit" a lot in the evening especially during breeding season. They are fond of being kept solitary. They tend to be very territorial, especially the males. The young ones are very secretive. On the other hand, adult frogs can become tame somehow.

Do Tomato frogs love to be handled?

Unlike cats and dogs, tomato frogs like the majority of the frogs do not enjoy being handled. It is advisable for you to handle your pet frog only when it is needed for instance, when you are going to clean its terrarium. Avoid unnecessary handling if, possible. Too much of it might cause stress to your frog. When you are handling your frog you may use protective gloves. The residue from your hand may actually infect your frog and the toxin it secretes can cause allergy or irritation to your skin. Therefore, it will be better if you're going to be wearing gloves for your pet's safety and yours as well.

What do they do when they feel threatened?

When they feel threatened or stressed, they secrete a white liquid substance. This is their defense mechanism against predators. The gooey liquid can actually cause skin irritation or allergy to humans. In some cases, Tomato frogs bite when they feel like they need to protect or defend themselves. As mentioned earlier, avoid unnecessary handling to prevent yourself from causing stress to your pet.

Do Tomato frogs bite?

Tomato frogs can be aggressive during feeding time or whenever they sense threat in the surroundings. There is a tendency that a Tomato frog will bite if it mistakenly took your fingers for food or if ever they feel that they are being threatened and need to defend themselves. You may use thongs in feeding it in order to avoid situations like the one mentioned.

What should I do when my Tomato Frog bite me?

The bite of Tomato frogs wouldn't cause serious damage but there may still be a need for you to clean up the wound if ever you got hurt. If ever your finger got stuck to its jaw and refuses to open its mouth, do not panic and stay calm. Do not pull your hand as it may cause damage to your frog's jaw. Instead, bring your frog under running water in order to encourage it to totally let go of your finger.

Facts about Tomato Frogs

Fact 1: Tomato frogs undergo the process of sloughing

There might be some instance that you will notice bits of skin inside your frog's cage. Do not worry since it is a natural circumstance that amphibians shed skin. If you see signs of skin shedding, you can try to mist your pet in order to make the shedding complete. When it has already peeled off, expect that your Tomato frog will eat it afterwards. This may sound disgusting but the skin that has been peeled of actually has some nutritional value beneficial for your pet.

Fact 2: Tomato frogs face estivation

Tomato frogs estivate during the dry season. Estivation is the term used to coin hibernation period. It is the process in which the frog form a cocoon of skin and mucus. It will burrow itself in mud or hide under plants. When the rainy season comes, it will come out from estivation and would eat for a few days. From then, it will proceed directly to breeding ponds and mate.

Fact 3: Tomato frogs do not need grooming

Unlike any other household pets, they should not be given baths or cleaned thoroughly with the use of bathing products as they can be potentially harmed or killed by these chemicals. Although they need no grooming, it is still necessary for you to maintain the cleanliness of your frog as well as its hygiene through properly cleaning and sanitizing its enclosure or terrarium.

Chapter Eight: Breeding Your Tomato Frogs

If you're planning to expand the family and ready to have froglets at home, it's now time for you to learn the basics of breeding a frog. Who knows? Maybe you'll become the most well-regarded frog breeder of all time. This part will really be helpful as you'll be provided with the topics like what sexual dimorphism is and how should you set up a breeding condition for your pet

Through this chapter, we'll help you identify the sex of your frog. You'll gain knowledge on how would you provide an ambiance for your pet in order for it to undergo the process of breeding.

Sexing

Before anything else, the first step you have to do in terms of breeding your Tomato frog is to be able to determine the sex of frogs. Unlike other animals, the sexual dimorphism of frogs can be very hard to determine since most frogs have their genitals internally. It can be a bit challenging but if you will pay close attention, you'll be able to do a successful frog sexing.

You may do this by observing the physical characteristics of your frog. Females appear larger and own a more brilliant color than males. Another way to determine whether your frog is a male or female is through the noise it makes. Usually, male frogs create a particular sound when they are finding for a mate during the breeding season. Through "calling", they can attract females who are ready to breed. If you find it hard to determine the sex of your frog, you may seek help from your veterinarian.

Breeding Basics

When you are going to breed your Tomato frogs there are some measures that you have to take. First you have to set up the correct environment for your frog. You must be able to mimic its natural habitat during the breeding season. Usually, frogs breed during rainy season. Most researchers agree that heavy rainfalls are what trigger Tomato frogs to breed. Make sure you'll provide the correct ambiance for your frog through setting up the correct environment with the use of manipulating its cage. You may cut down misting and lower the temperature of your frog's cage for about 5 degrees Fahrenheit. Then after a month, return the normal level of its required temperature and heavily mist the terrarium and provide plenty of food for them. This way you are able to simulate seasonal changes to your pet.

Before the breeding begins, your Tomato frog will undergo the process of estivation or hibernation. Usually, they burrow themselves under mud or moss and they may also hide behind plants. You may start to reduce humidity level and temperature when you have observed that your pet frog has been staying under its substrate longer that it usually does. Make sure that your frog has access to water during this period.

When your frog is ready, it will go out from its hiding place and for a few days it will eat a lot. After that, it will be ready for mating.

Male frogs would do vocalization in order to call out for its mate. If it has already found one the mating will begin. Make sure to provide plants so that your female frogs will be able to attach its eggs on it inside the terrarium.

Spawning

The term spawning is used to coin the term hatching for frogs. Expect that a female Tomato Frog can produce 1500 eggs per clutch. When it has already laid the eggs, immediately separate it from your adult frog as it has the tendency to eat its offspring. Each egg comes in the size not larger than 2 mm. It might take 36 hours before the eggs will hatch. By that period, you must provide additional water inside the cage.

Tadpole Maintenance

Taking care of tadpoles can really be a challenge and so you must be very sure that you are ready to breed your frog. After the hatching of eggs, tadpoles will emerge. The stage of being a tadpole usually last for 7 to 9 weeks. They feed on tiny bits of nutrients found in water through the use of filtration. In general, they are cannibals and so it is recommended that you will put them into separate jars as they have the tendency to eat each other once they are placed on the same enclosure. Make sure to clean the jars before putting them in it.

You may also provide a separate cage filled with live plants. There is a tendency that you might lose a number of tadpoles but still, this can be more convenient for you especially when you are about to feed them.

You may sprinkle finely-ground fish food for your tadpoles. Make sure that you will be able to maintain the quality of the water inside the enclosure by changing it occasionally through the use of an aerator to prevent old food from lingering in the cage.

Tadpole Metamorphosis

As tadpoles mature, they will begin to face changes in terms of their body structure. The period of apoptosis will take place or the process on which cells die and cause the reabsorption of the organs or body parts of the tadpoles that are considered redundant. Their gills will eventually disappear as their lungs develop. They will have thicker and tougher skin, its tail will disappear as their legs develop, and many more changes in appearance. After this stage, they will become juvenile frog or baby frogs. Make sure to remove the water from its enclosure and provide them the same set up as what you did to an adult frog's terrarium.

You may feed young ones with wingless fruit flies and small crickets. Make sure that you will provide the correct husbandry to these little ones.

How to Become a Successful Breeder

In order to become a successful breeder, you must dedicate your time and effort. If ever the breeding wasn't successful, do not get frustrated. Accept the fact that not all frog mating leads to a success in producing eggs. Make sure you will be able to provide all the things needed by your pet from the environment down to the specific care it requires. Make sure that you will be hands on during the period of breeding. For a bigger chance of a successful breeding, it will be better for you to have a higher ratio of frog rather than having one pair as competition is believed to encourage breeding. A larger number of males compared to females can cause the males to become more active and energetic for breeding.

Chapter Nine: Common Diseases and Treatments for Tomato Frogs

Tomato frogs are generally healthy but it doesn't mean that they are a hundred percent immune on catching any illnesses; having said that, you must be aware and regularly observe your pet. If it looks lethargic and seems losing its appetite brings it immediately to the vet as these are the common signs that your pet is sick.

In this chapter, you'll learn about the common health problems Tomato frogs might potentially face along with the treatment that may be administered in order to bring back the health of your pet to its best state. Being knowledgeable about this will help you save your pet's life and your wallet from spending bucks as well.

Common Health Problems

Tomato frogs are healthy species in general but they have the potential of carrying and becoming infected with certain diseases. It is very important for you to know the common health problems that your frog might face. If ever your frog is acting weird and showing signs of being ill, do not hesitate and bring it immediately to your veterinarian. Before we let you know what diseases is common for Tomato frogs we'll give you first some points on how to prevent your pet from have such illnesses.

Selection

Selection is where it all starts. Be observant when you are choosing your frog. Make sure that you will be able to pick out a hardy one. Usually, a jumpy frog is a healthy frog. Check for any signs of abnormalities in bone structure, deformation, and skinniness for these might indicate malnutrition. Check if the eyes are free from any discharge. As much as possible, it is your target to bring home a healthy frog.

Transportation

Bringing your pet home can bring stress to your pet. It is best that you'll be able to put your frog in a secure place wherein it will not bump into walls when it panics. Make sure that as you transport them, they will feel comfortable.

Quarantine

In order for you to be sure that your frog is free from any diseases, you should have it quarantined. This process can also help you prevent the spread of disease if ever the frog you have purchased is carrying a transmittable disease. Keep your frog in a separate tank for at least 45 days. Have its fecal matter be tested as well.

Water

In order to keep your frog healthy, make sure that it is properly hydrated. Provide it with de-chlorinated water. Ensure that the water bowl of your pet will be refilled regularly.

Food

Provide your pet with food with high nutritional value. It is recommended that you provide them gut-loaded crickets. Dust the food you are going to serve with calcium powder and other multivitamins as well. You may ask your veterinarian with regard to the supplements you should administer to your pet

Handling

When you are handling your pet, make sure that you have washed your hands first. Handle it gently and carefully. When it panics when you are about to touch it, do not pursue and let it relax. This might happen on the first week of its stay in its new habitat. Wait until your frog become familiar with you when it has already fully adjusted well with the whole surrounding

Common Conditions Affecting Tomato Frogs

Metabolic Bone Disease (MBD)

Metabolic Bone Disease also known as MBD is a complex illness not only for tomato frogs but to all kinds of frogs as well. This causes the weakening of the bones. Active frogs are generally the ones who likely break their bones as they hop or hunt for food. This may result to crippling or in extreme scenarios, death.

This is not only caused by a Calcium of Vitamin D3 deficiency. It is actually a calcium metabolism disorder. Some frogs are not able to absorb calcium and transform it into its useable form. Low calcium level results to soft bones which makes your pet more vulnerable on having fractures. The disability to absorb Vitamin D is also one of the factors that trigger this orthopedic disease.

Symptoms:

During the early stage, Metabolic Bone Disease is less likely to be detected. Symptoms include the following:

- Bumps found on its vertebral column/ arched spine

- Swollen or flimsy legs

- Swelling of the jaw

- Softening of the jaw

- Lower jaw has receded

- Weakness

- Constipation

- Little movements

- Lethargy

- Anorexia

- Bone fractures

- Partial Paralysis

- Loss of body mass

- Shakiness when being held

- Jerky manner when walking

- Twitching of muscles in the limbs and legs even at rest

Treatment

Unfortunately, this disease cannot be reversed but its progression can be stopped through gut-loading its meal with calcium and Vitamin D3 rich food. If ever you have saw the signs that your pet might have MBD, immediately bring it to you veterinarian. Your vet might recommend you to administer calcium with D3 directly on its mouth at least every day or every other day depending on its severity.

Red-leg Syndrome

This illness is common to toads, frogs, and even salamanders. It is defined by the redness on the frog's legs and abdomen. This is usually caused by a bacterial pathogen called Aeromonas hydrophila. Viruses and fungi can also cause the redness.

Symptoms:

The symptoms of the Red-leg Syndrome are the following:

- Lethargy

- Anemia

- Drastic weight loss

- Ascitis or accumulation of fluid in the abdominal cavity

Treatment

Bring your pet immediately to the veterinarian when your pet is showing the signs of this illness. Be careful not to mistaken the redness of the legs from its natural color. Your pet might undergo series of tests like blood tests or body fluid tests in order to detect if it's really infected.

Fungal Infection

Fungal infections are common with tadpoles and aquatic amphibians.

Symptoms:

The symptoms for fungal infection are as follows:

- Abnormality in skin color

- Red Inflammation

Treatment

If it is during the early stage of fungal infection you may treat it with the use of a 2% solution of malachite green or mercurochrome. Immerse your frog in the solution for at least 5 minutes. Repeat the process if the symptoms do not improve. You may also bring your pet to the vet for medical care.

Chapter Ten: Care Sheet and Summary

Congratulations! You have reached the final chapter of this book. I hope you have learned so much from everything that we have discussed. This may be the last but definitely not the least chapter. In this phase, you'll be provided with a summary of everything that has been discussed in the prior chapters. If ever you are in a hurry and would like to check out a specific information or topic you can easily locate it here without the need to go over and read the whole book.

We hope that you wouldn't stop finding ways on how you'll be able to take care of your pet properly. We hope that you would dedicate your time in order to learn more about this specie and how to become a responsible owner. It has been a great opportunity in helping you gain knowledge with regard to Tomato frogs.

Biological Information

Taxonomy: Tomato Frogs have a scientific name of Dyscophus antongilii .They belong in Kingdom *Animalia,* Phylum *Chordata*, Class *Amphibia*, Order *Anura* Family *Microhylidae*, Genus *Dyscophus,* and Species *antongilii/ guneti/ insularis*

Country of Origin: The natural range of Tomato Frogs is located exclusively on the island of Madagascar down the east coast of Africa.

Size: Adult males can grow as large as 2.5 inches while females can grow and reach 4 inches measuring from snout to vent.

Body Type and Appearance: Their forefeet are not webbed and their hind limbs 'webbing is not that pronounced.

Color: Females come in a bright red-orange while males have a duller skin that ranges from yellow-orange to brownish-orange similar to the color of a tomato fruit.

Usually, their bellies are yellowish and there are instances that their back and throat have black spots.

Defense Mechanism: When they are under a threat, they secrete glue like substance as an act to deter predators. This can actually produce allergic reactions to human skin.

Lifespan: They can live an average life of 6 years

Sub – Species of Tomato Frogs:

Dyscophus antongilii - Madagascar Tomato Frog

Its body possess an orange-red color which is strikingly vibrant. Females are a lot larger than males. Usually, males have a dull color compared to the skin of the females. Its color act as a warning, that they can be toxic for their potential predators. When they are under a threat, they secrete glue like substance as an act to deter predators.

Dyscophus guineti - False Tomato Frog

They exhibit a bright and attractive red-orange color giving life to where its name has been derived from. When they are stressed, they secrete a white liquid substance. This is their defense mechanism whenever a predator comes in their way. This can be deadly to others but can only bring allergy to human skin.

Dyscophus Insularis

This is a medium-sized terrestrial frog. Unlike other tomato frogs, their color is brown-greyish which are usually symmetrical and has darker markings. Males have a dark vocal sac. Be careful since whenever they are stressed, they secrete this substance which can bring allergic reactions to your skin.

Requirements for Tomato Frogs

If you have the plan to purchase a Tomato frog, you must be knowledgeable not only on their characteristics but also to the certain regulations or restrictions that you have to observe in order to keep them legally.

CITES Laws for Frogs

What is CITES?

CITES or the Convention on International Trade in Endangered Species for wild fauna and flora is the one responsible for taking care of plants and animals of different species especially the ones who are considered as endangered. Majority of the countries belonging in the major continents in the world like Europe, USA, Latin

America, Australia, and Asia have become a part of the organization.

What composes CITES?

- Appendix I is composed of species that are considered as most endangered among any other animals and plants listed by CITES.
- Appendix II is a list of species that are not necessarily threatened with extinction.
- Appendix III is full of species requested by different parties that regulate trade in the species

Frog Licensing: It is advisable for you to have your frog licensed to save you in case of any trouble. Sometime there are veterinarians who checks on the license of the pet in order for them to ensure that you are keeping your pet legally.

Requirements for Licensing: In general, you don't need to have approval from wildlife organizations or authorities in order to have your frog licensing. All you have to do is to provide a document with the name, identity of the specie on which your frog belongs. There is a need for you to give information like name, address, contact details, and the signature of the previous owner or on where you bought your frog is also needed. You also have to provide your personal information and contact information

Costs

Purchase Price: $20 - $50

The cost of a Tomato frog varies. Its price actually depends on its age, color, availability and the breed or specie it belongs to. If you want to purchase a frog with a lower cost you may transact with backyard breeder but at your own risk since if you're going to acquire frogs from them, you wouldn't be so sure that the frogs are well-taken care of or if they are really a captive-bred or have just been randomly captured in the wild.

Terrarium and Screen Lid: $20- $40

A frog needs its own place to stay in order to feel relaxed, safe, and comfortable. It is ideal for you to mimic its natural habitat for it to be able to adjust easily on its new surroundings. In buying a cage, make sure that it is appropriate for the size and age of your frog. The enclosure should be made out of glass so that you can easily monitor your pet, regulate temperature, and for the reason that this kind of cage will be easier to clean.

Food, Water Dish, Tank Heater: $20- $35

Tomato frogs can be fed by gut-loaded cricket. There is also a need for their food to be dusted with calcium powder as they need the mineral for them to avoid developing certain diseases. Therefore, tank heater along with thermometer and hygrometer will be needed.

Veterinarian Consultations: $75- $100 or more

It is advisable for your pet to visit the vet once in a while for a routine check-up in order to make sure that its health is exceptional. And so, you need to save up for its medical needs and veterinarian costs. You should also save a budget for medical or lab tests just in case your frog will need such procedures

Supplies/Accessories: $10- $15

In order to simulate a healthy environment for your pet, you should be able to set up its terrarium as if it's living in the wild. You may add cage decors such as branches, leaves, live plants, moss and other things that would make the cage pleasing to the eyes.

UVB Lighting and Gauges: $50 and up

It is not really that necessary for Tomato frogs to have access on UVB Lighting but having one won't hurt. UV lighting is not really required for Tomato frogs but using one would benefit your pet as it can help the frog process calcium and other vitamins that are beneficial for its health.

Purchasing and Selecting a Healthy Breed

Where to Purchase: Backyard Breeders, Local Pet Stores, Amphibian Conventions

Steps in Finding a Reputable Breeder:

Step 1: Investigate: Detective mode on! Bring out your magnifying glasses as we are going to make a little investigation towards the breeder you are about to deal with. Doing a background check is the initial step. Check the content of the website. Make sure the complete contact information as well as the facilities of the breeder is shown.

If the website of the breeder seems suspicious, leave the site and just find another legitimate breeder.

Step 2: Interview: You may try to contact the breeder through phone and conduct an interview. You may ask for their experience with regard to taking care of a Tomato Frog and how long they have been breeding Tomato frogs. One great sign that the breeder you are having a conversation with a reputable breeder is when he ask about you as well. A good breeder would ensure that the frog he bred will be transferred into good hands,

Step 3: Inspect: You may request for an ocular visit inside the facilities of the breeder. If he allows you to do so, it means that they aren't hiding anything and confident that he is taking care of the Tomato frogs well. Inspect the area where the frogs have been raised. Make sure that it is clean and pleasant. If the environment seems unhygienic and unorganized, do not deal the breeder.

Characteristics of a Healthy Breed:

- The skin should be bright and clean.
- It shouldn't have scratches, lumps, dryness, and irritations. The eyes should be clean and free from any haziness or cloudiness as these may indicate a disease.
- It should be active.

- Signs of being bloated, lethargic, and lazy should not be present.
- The frog should look enthusiastic.
- It should be able to eat properly during "feeding time."

Habitat Requirements for Tomato Frogs:

Cage - For every Tomato frog you own, you must provide a 10-gallon aquarium. Although this size of enclosure can house two adult Tomato frogs, it is still advisable for you to provide a larger one if you are letting them live together. For tadpoles, provide them a glass terrarium with a screen lid on the top.

Hiding Spot - Make sure you'll be able to provide a hiding place for your frog. You may use a half-branch log tunnels that can be bought in local pet stores. Ensure that the size of the hiding spot is appropriate for you frog.

Accessories and Accents - It is very important that you'll be able to mimic the natural habitat of Tomato frogs. Adding plants can keep your pet feel secure and comfortable. You may add fake plants or even real plants such as Pothos.

Water Bowl - A water bowl is essential for your frog's hydration. You should provide a large but shallow water bowl for your Tomato frog. Its depth should not be higher than the height of your pet when resting in order to avoid the risk of drowning.

Temperature - The temperature inside the cage should be maintained at 75 to 85 degrees Fahrenheit during the day and 65-75 degrees Fahrenheit during night time. Always keep track of temperatures because when it reaches higher than 80 degrees Fahrenheit, it might cause the death of your frog.

Humidity - Humidity can be maintained through the process of misting the enclosure twice daily- in the morning and during the afternoon. The humidity level of the cage should be 70% to 80%. The best way to measure humidity is through a digital hygrometer.

Lighting - Although lighting is not essential for tomato frogs, there is still a need for you to install spectrum bulbs such as fluorescent tubes in order for the live plants to grow.

Nutritional Requirements

Primary diet: small roaches, crickets, silkworms, night crawlers, horn worms, and other types of insects and worms. They can also eat rodents. It is recommended that the meal you provide for your pet varies for a more balanced nutrition.

Feeding Amount for Tomato Frogs: Juveniles or the younger frogs should be fed for 5 to 7 times a week, on the other hand, adults should be fed for 3 to 4 times a week or every other day. The amount of food you should serve depends on the size of your tomato frog. For tadpoles and young frogs, there is a diet called gut-loaded diet that you may want to administer in order to strengthen the body of your pet as well as its immune system against any illnesses as it grows.

How to Feed Tomato Frogs:

- **Check the nutritional value:** Make sure that you are providing the best food for your pet. See to it that they will receive enough vitamins and minerals

- **Gut-load the prey:** If you are going to feed your frog with insects, it is advisable that you gut load its food first with ingredients that is high in calcium and low in phosphorus, goitrogens, and oxalates.

- **Establish Meal Schedules:** Be sure that you are following the right schedule when to feed your tomato frog

- **Do not overfeed:** Make sure that the amount of food you are providing for your frog would only be enough. Do not overfeed it as it may cause several digestive problems.

- **Use thong if you aren't used to touching insects:** It is under your discretion if you are going to hand-feed your frog. If you aren't comfortable with handling insects, you may use thong s or any other tools in feeding your pet.

Lifecycle of Tomato Frogs

Reproduction - In some breeding programs for captive-breds, males are found to be calling and amplexing females under simulated heavy rainstorms just like what they use to have in Madagascar. After calling out for mates and finding a match, the male will cling to the female or will undergo the so-called amplexing. After that you may expect 1500 eggs per clutch. Eggs that have been fertilized will be deposited on stagnant water or in small ponds. It may take up to 36 hours before these eggs hatch.

The Eggs or Frogspawn - The eggs are enclosed in a jelly-like substance which protects them until they hatch. It is usually sticky and comes into a black and white color. They will fall directly to stagnant water or small ponds and will look like a film over the surface of the water. Each egg comes in the size not larger than 2 mm. After 3 days, these fertilized eggs will turn into small tadpoles. The more eggs the frog lays, the more chances that some of them will survive.

Larvae or Tadpoles - Tadpoles are only a half centimetre in length making them a welcome prey for animals larger than them. They resemble so much of a fish's physique as they also use their tails for swimming and their gills for breathing. This stage will usually last for 7 to 9 weeks. They feed on tiny bits of nutrients found in water through the use of filtration. As they mature, they will develop small legs that will help them emerge from water and crawl towards the land

Froglets or Young Frogs - Small Tomato frogs or froglets are somewhat yellow in color. This stage is where they become terrestrial species and explore the environment outside water. Their body size will gradually increase as time goes by.

Adult Frogs- It takes almost a year before a frog totally matures but in the case of a female Tomato frog, it takes a minimum of 2 years before it becomes a fully-grown adult. When this happens you can easily see the difference through its color and size. Females grow larger than male. They can grow up to 4 inches while an adult male can grow as large as 2.5 inches.

Caring Guidelines for Tomato Frogs

How do Tomato frogs behave in general? - Tomato frogs, in general, are calm and easy going frogs. They are nocturnal which means they are most active during nigh time. They are considered as one of the noisiest types of frogs. They tend to be very territorial, especially the males. The young ones are very secretive. On the other hand, adult frogs can become tame somehow.

Do Tomato frogs love to be handled? - Unlike cats and dogs, tomato frogs like the majority of the frogs do not enjoy being handled. It is advisable for you to handle your pet frog only when it is needed for instance, when you are going to clean its terrarium.

What do they do when they feel threatened? - When they feel threatened or stressed, they secrete a white liquid substance. This is their defense mechanism against predators. The gooey liquid can actually cause skin irritation or allergy to humans.

Do Tomato frogs bite? - Tomato frogs can be aggressive during feeding time or whenever they sense threat in the surroundings. There is a tendency that a Tomato frog will bite if it mistakenly took your fingers for food or if ever they feel that they are being threatened and need to defend themselves.

What should I do when my Tomato Frog bit me?

The bite of Tomato frogs wouldn't cause serious damage but there may still be a need for you to clean up the wound if ever you got hurt. If ever your finger got stuck to its jaw and refuses to open its mouth, do not panic and stay calm. Bring your frog under running water in order to encourage it to totally let go of your finger.

Fact 1: Tomato frogs undergo the process of sloughing - If you see signs of skin shedding, you can try to mist your pet in order to make the shedding complete. When it has already peeled off, expect that your Tomato frog will eat it afterwards

Fact 2: Tomato frogs face estivation - Tomato frogs estivate during the dry season. Estivation is the term used to coin hibernation period. It is the process in which the frog forms a cocoon of skin and mucus. It will burrow itself in mud or hide under plants.

Fact 3: Tomato frogs do not need grooming - Unlike any other household pets, they should not be given baths or cleaned thoroughly with the use of bathing products as they can be potentially harmed or killed by these chemicals. Although they need no grooming, it is still necessary for you to maintain the cleanliness of your frog as well as its hygiene through properly cleaning and sanitizing its enclosure or terrarium.

Breeding Your Tomato Frog

Sexing: You may determine the sex of frogs by observing the physical characteristics of your frog. Females appear larger and own a more brilliant color than males. Another way to determine whether your frog is a male or female is through the noise it makes. Usually, male frogs create a particular sound when they are finding for a mate during the breeding season.

Breeding Basics: You must be able to mimic its natural habitat during the breeding season. You may cut down misting and lower the temperature of your frog's cage for about 5 degrees Fahrenheit. Then after a month, return the normal level of its required temperature and heavily mist the terrarium and provide plenty of food for them. This way you are able to simulate seasonal changes to your pet.

Spawning: Expect that a female Tomato Frog can produce 1500 eggs per clutch. When it has already laid the eggs, immediately separate it from your adult frog as it has the tendency to eat its offspring. It might take 36 hours before the eggs will hatch.

Tadpole Metamorphosis: The stage of being a tadpole usually last for 7 to 9 weeks. They feed on tiny bits of nutrients found in water through the use of filtration. In general, they are cannibals and so it is recommended that you will put them into separate jars. You may also provide a separate cage filled with live plants. You may sprinkle finely-ground fish food for your tadpoles.

Tadpole Maintenance: The period of apoptosis will take place or the process on which cells die and cause the reabsorption of the organs or body parts of the tadpoles that are considered redundant. After this stage, they will become juvenile frog or baby frogs. Make sure to remove the water from its enclosure and provide them the same set up as what you did to an adult frog's terrarium

How to become a successful breeder: You must dedicate your time and effort and make sure you will be able to provide all the things needed by your pet from the environment down to the specific care it requires.

Common Diseases and Health Requirements

Metabolic Bone Disease (MBD)

Metabolic Bone Disease also known as MBD is a complex illness not only for tomato frogs but to all kinds of frogs as well. This causes the weakening of the bones. This is not only caused by a Calcium of Vitamin D3 deficiency. It is actually a calcium metabolism disorder. The disability to absorb Vitamin D is also one of the factors that trigger this orthopedic disease.

Symptoms

- Bumps found on its vertebral column/ arched spine

- Swollen or flimsy legs

- Swelling of the jaw

- Softening of the jaw

- Lower jaw has receded

- Weakness

- Constipation

- Little movements

- Lethargy

- Anorexia

- Bone fractures

- Partial Paralysis

- Loss of body mass

- Shakiness when being held

- Jerky manner when walking

- Twitching of muscles in the limbs and legs even at rest

Treatment

Unfortunately, this disease cannot be reversed but its progression can be stopped through gut-loading its meal with calcium and Vitamin D3 rich food. If ever you have saw the signs that your pet might have MBD, immediately bring it to you veterinarian.

Red-leg Syndrome

It is defined by the redness on the frog's legs and abdomen. This is usually caused by a bacterial pathogen called Aeromonas hydrophila. Viruses and fungi can also cause the redness.

Symptoms

- Lethargy
- Anemia
- Drastic weight loss
- Ascitis or accumulation of fluid in the abdominal cavity

Treatment

Bring your pet immediately to the veterinarian when your pet is showing the signs of this illness. Your pet might undergo series of tests like blood tests or body fluid tests in order to detect if it's really infected.

Fungal Infection

Fungal infections are common with tadpoles and aquatic amphibian

Symptoms

- Abnormality in skin color
- Red Inflammation

Treatment

If it is during the early stage of fungal infection you may treat it with the use of a 2% solution of malachite green or mercurochrome.

Glossary of Frog Terms

Advertisement Call - Males frogs' and toads' mating call

Aggressive Call- Territorial Call; it is a call made by male when another male comes too close

Amphibian- double life; animals that are vertebrates and lives a part of their lives in water

Amplexus- A position wherein the male frog is on the top of a female in order to externally fertilize the eggs

Anura- tail-less; the order of toads and frogs

Archaeobatrachia- ancient frogs

Army- a collective term used to define a group of frogs

Aquatic- lives in water

Bask- to sit under the sunlight in order to warm up

Beaufort Wind Scale- a kind of scale used to monitor and estimate the speed of the wind

Binomial Nomenclature- biological name assigned to every living thing

Boss- an area on the toad's head between the eyes that is raised

Carnivore- species that eat meat

Chorus- a large group of singing, calling toads and/or frogs

Chytridiomycosis (BD) - Chytrid; a fungus of frogs that affects their skin's permeability

CITES- The Convention on International Train Endangered Species of wild fauna and flora

Citizen Scientists- citizens who contribute scientific information for various researches and projects worldwide

Cold-blooded- Ectothermic

Detritus- decaying animal matter and plant settling at the bottom of the pond

Digits- toes or fingers

Distress call- a call made by a frog or toad in order to discourage a predator

Dorsal- upper side

Dorsolateral- stripes or parallel folds along the back of a frog

Ecosystem- the interaction between the environment and living organisms

Ectothermic- the ability of a specie to control its body temperature through the use of available surroundings

Genera- related species that share the same first name

Habitat- it is where plant, animals, and other species live and grow

Herbivore- a specie that feeds on plant

Herpetologist- a scientist who studies amphibians and reptiles

Herpetology- The study of Amphibians and Reptiles

Insectivore- a specie that feeds on insect

Invasive Species- species that are not native to an area and cause ecological harm

Invertebrate- a specie without a backbone

Knot- a group of toads

Lateral- side surface

Mesobatrachia- Middle Frogs

Metamorphosis- stages of change that a specie undergo

Nictating Membrane- inner eyelid which is transparent

Paratoid glands- toxin glands found behind the eyes of toads

Phenology- Study of the Seasonal Timing of Events

Polyplois- having one or more than one sets of chromosomes

Pollywog- tadpole

Pupil- part of the eye on which the light enters

Ranavirus- a kind of disease of amphibians

Release call- a call made by a female when she's not yet ready or a call made by a male if another male thought he's a female

Spawn- eggs of frogs and toads

Submerged- beneath the surface

Tadpole- a frog's larval stage

Taxonomy- classifying all living things based on their similarities and differences

Territorial Call- Aggressive Call

Tibial gland- a gland found on the lower leg

Toe Pads- sticky area on the toes

Tubercle- Rough area on a toad's body

Tympanum- eardrum

Ventral- refers to the lower surface of the body or belly

Vernal Pools- Temporary ponds that are filled with water seasonally as the snow melts or when it rains

Vocal sac- an expandable sac found beneath the frog/toad's throat

Wetland- wet area between deep water and uplands

A

B

C

D

S

T

V

W

Photo Credits

Page 1 Photo by user Francesco Veronesi via Flickr.com, https://www.flickr.com/photos/francesco_veronesi/15111422549/

Page 3 Photo by user Ettore Balocchi via Flickr.com, https://www.flickr.com/photos/29882791@N02/8302379461/

Page 10 Photo by user Michael Sale via Flickr.com, https://www.flickr.com/photos/michaelsale/10268579663/

Page 20 Photo by user Josh More via Flickr.com, https://www.flickr.com/photos/guppiecat/8636514526/

Page 30 Photo by user Brian Gatwicke via Flickr.com, https://www.flickr.com/photos/briangratwicke/15284643444/

Page 38 Photo by user Heather Paul via Flickr.com, https://www.flickr.com/photos/warriorwoman531/8328079065/

Page 48 Photo by user Bernard DUPONT via Flickr.com, https://www.flickr.com/photos/berniedup/9674666202/

Page 54 Photo by user Josh More via Flickr.com,

https://www.flickr.com/photos/guppiecat/27491682626/

Page 60 Photo by user Niharb Natalie via Flickr.com,
https://www.flickr.com/photos/nbhattac/4062301853/

Page 66 Photo by user Josh More via Flickr.com,
https://www.flickr.com/photos/guppiecat/8636514404/

Page 74 Photo by user MantellaMan via Flickr.com,
https://www.flickr.com/photos/109773582@N04/11252100874
/

References

"Blog About Frogs" Blogaboutfrogs.blogspot.com

<http://blogaboutfrogs.blogspot.com/2010/12/signs-of-healthy-frog.html/>

"Differences Between a Male and a Female Frog" Cuteness.com

<https://www.cuteness.com/article/differences-between-male-female-frog/>

"Frog Diseases: Metabolic Bone Disease (MBD) Frogworld.net

<http://frogworld.net/health/mbd.html/>

"Frog Shedding" Frogforum.net

<http://www.frogforum.net/showthread.php/23736-Tomato-frog-Shedding/>

"How to Breed Frogs" Wikihow.com

<https://www.wikihow.com/Breed-Frogs/>

"The IUCN Red List of Threatened Species"Iucnredlist.org

<http://www.iucnredlist.org/details/6937/0/>

"Tomato Frog" Regalpet.com

<https://regalpet.com/pets/735-tomato-frog/>

"Tomato Frog Care" Wilmettepetcenter.com

<http://wilmettepetcenter.com/2011/10/16/tomato-frog-care/>

" Tomato Frog Care Sheet" Clubfauna.com

<http://www.clubfauna.com/articles/amphibians/tomato-frog-care-sheet/>

"
Tomato Frog Care Sheet" Reptilesmagazine.com

<http://www.reptilesmagazine.com/Care-Sheets/Frogs-Amphibians/Tomato-Frog/>

"Tomato Frogs" Allaboutfrogs.org

<http://allaboutfrogs.org/info/species/tomato.html/>

"Tomato Frogs" Nationalzoo.si.edu

<https://nationalzoo.si.edu/animals/tomato-frog Tomato Frogs/>

Feeding Baby
Cynthia Cherry
978-1941070000

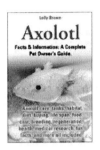

Axolotl
Lolly Brown
978-0989658430

Dysautonomia, POTS
Syndrome
Frederick Earlstein
978-0989658485

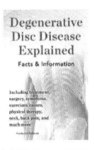

Degenerative Disc
Disease Explained
Frederick Earlstein
978-0989658485

Sinusitis, Hay Fever,
Allergic Rhinitis Explained
Frederick Earlstein
978-1941070024

Wicca
Riley Star
978-1941070130

Zombie Apocalypse
Rex Cutty
978-1941070154

Capybara
Lolly Brown
978-1941070062

Eels As Pets
Lolly Brown
978-1941070167

Scabies and Lice Explained
Frederick Earlstein
978-1941070017

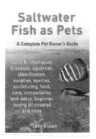

Saltwater Fish As Pets
Lolly Brown
978-0989658461

Torticollis Explained
Frederick Earlstein
978-1941070055

Kennel Cough
Lolly Brown
978-0989658409

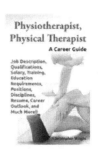

Physiotherapist, Physical
Therapist
Christopher Wright
978-0989658492

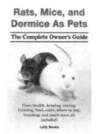

Rats, Mice, and Dormice
As Pets
Lolly Brown
978-1941070079

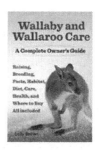

Wallaby and Wallaroo Care
Lolly Brown
978-1941070031

Bodybuilding Supplements
Explained
Jon Shelton
978-1941070239

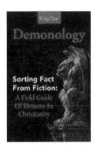

Demonology
Riley Star
978-19401070314

Pigeon Racing
Lolly Brown
978-1941070307

Dwarf Hamster
Lolly Brown
978-1941070390

Cryptozoology
Rex Cutty
978-1941070406

Eye Strain
Frederick Earlstein
978-1941070369

Inez The Miniature Elephant
Asher Ray
978-1941070353

Vampire Apocalypse
Rex Cutty
978-1941070321

Made in the USA
San Bernardino, CA
07 May 2019